PSALMS PATH

CO-CREATING RIGHTEOUS DESIRES WITH GOD
FOR THE PURPOSE OF GOING FROM CHRISTIAN TO
EFFECTIVE DISCIPLE OF JESUS

RUSTY ROBERTS

Trilogy Christian Publishers
A Wholly Owned Subsidiary of Trinity Broadcasting Network
2442 Michelle Drive
Tustin, CA 92780
Copyright © 2024 by Rusty Roberts
Scripture quotations marked NKJV are taken from the New King James Version®. Copyright © 1982 by Thomas Nelson. Used by permission. All rights reserved.
Scripture quotations marked NIV are taken from the Holy Bible, New International Version®, NIV®. Copyright © 1973, 1978, 1984, 2011 by Biblica, Inc.™ Used by permission of Zondervan. All rights reserved worldwide. www.zondervan.com. The "NIV" and "New International Version" are trademarks registered in the United States Patent and Trademark Office by Biblica, Inc.™ Scripture quotations marked KJV are taken from the King James Version of the Bible. Public domain. Scripture quotations marked NASB are taken from the New American Standard Bible® (NASB), Copyright © 1960, 1962, 1963, 1968, 1971, 1972, 1973, 1975, 1977, 1995 by The Lockman Foundation. Used by permission. www.Lockman.org. Scripture quotations marked NLT are taken from the Holy Bible, New Living Translation, copyright © 1996, 2004, 2015 by Tyndale House Foundation. Used by permission of Tyndale House Publishers, Inc., Carol Stream, Illinois 60188. All rights reserved. Scripture quotations marked RSV are taken from the Revised Standard Version of the Bible, copyright © 1946, 1952, and 1971 the Division of Christian Education of the National Council of the Churches of Christ in the United States of America. Used by permission. All rights reserved.
All rights reserved, including the right to reproduce this book or portions thereof in any form whatsoever.
For information, address Trilogy Christian Publishing
Rights Department, 2442 Michelle Drive, Tustin, CA 92780.
Trilogy Christian Publishing/ TBN and colophon are trademarks of Trinity Broadcasting Network.
For information about special discounts for bulk purchases, please contact Trilogy Christian Publishing.
Trilogy Disclaimer: The views and content expressed in this book are those of the author and may not necessarily reflect the views and doctrine of Trilogy Christian Publishing or the Trinity Broadcasting Network.
10 9 8 7 6 5 4 3 2 1
Library of Congress Cataloging-in-Publication Data is available.
ISBN 979-8-89333-436-4
ISBN 979-8-89333-437-1 (ebook)

TABLE OF CONTENTS

Foreword to *Psalms Path* by Sean Murphy 5
My Psalms Path Journey 7
The Making of My Righteous Desire 9
Introduction 13
The Psalms Path 14
Chapter 1: Co-Creators with God 15
Chapter 2: 5 Criteria for Righteous Desires: 19
Chapter 3: Your Daily Duties 25
Chapter 4: Satan Will Try to Kill Your Righteous Desire 31
Chapter 5: Reality Check 35
Chapter 6: Circumstances That Could Occur
When Walking the Psalms Path 37
Chapter 7: Psalms Path Verses 1, 2, 3, 6, 7, 8
with Supporting Scriptures 43
Chapter 8: Don't Waste the Wait 47
Chapter 9: Why Would the Lord Allow Us to
Co-Create Righteous Desires? 55
Chapter 10: Concluding Questions and Answers 59
Chapter 11: Enlightened Transcendence 71

FOREWORD TO *PSALMS PATH* BY SEAN MURPHY

In the winter of 2022, as I closed the doors to my gym for the last time, little did I know that God was setting the stage for an extraordinary chapter in my life. My journey from that moment of uncertainty to where I stand today is a testament to divine timing and the transformative power of faith. It was during this period of transition, as I poured my heart into an online ministry, that I crossed paths with Rusty—a meeting I now recognize as a divine introduction.

It was in February of 2023 that Rusty introduced me to the principles of the "Psalms Path," which have since become a cornerstone of my daily reflection and growth. Centered around the profound wisdom of Psalm 37:1-8, these insights offered not just solace but a blueprint for navigating life's uncertainties with faith and purpose. I eagerly scribbled its title on my whiteboard, and those passages became my daily bread, nourishing my soul and guiding my steps.

As I walked the "Psalms Path," my life began to unfold in ways I had never imagined. From a fledgling online ministry, I witnessed my following burgeon to over 150,000 souls, each interaction woven into the fabric of a growing community of faith. My conversations with Rusty, though miles apart, were bridges connecting me to a larger purpose, revealing opportunities I had never dared to dream of. Partnerships, coaching roles, content creation for a Christian non-profit organization, sharing my testimony, both online and recently, through my first public speaking event at a church, and now, the journey of penning my own book—each milestone was a stone laid on the path paved by the wisdom of Psalm 37.

Psalms Path is more than a book; it is a gateway to transformation and fulfillment. Its teachings, deeply rooted in biblical principles, serve as a beacon for all who seek to align their entrepreneurial spirit with God's divine purpose. My story, a single thread in the tapestry of faith, bears witness to the profound impact of living by the guidance found within these pages.

As you turn these pages, I invite you to journey with an open heart. May *Psalms Path* illuminate your way, as it did mine, guiding you toward a life of purpose, abundance, and unwavering faith. Herein lies not just a pathway to entrepreneurial success but a call to walk in the righteousness and peace of God's promise.

With heartfelt conviction and the deepest faith,
Sean Murphy

MY PSALMS PATH JOURNEY

When God granted my righteous desire, I was spiritually unprepared, resulting in daily fretting and intense fear from 2019 to 2022.

Reflecting on the past, I now realize that the Lord permitted a two-year waiting period (from 2017 to 2019) for the desire to come to fruition, intending for me to utilize that time for adequate preparation. Unfortunately, I failed to do so, and when the window of opportunity opened, I found myself enduring two and a half harrowing years filled with daily fretting. This tumultuous period culminated in a perilous experience that nearly drove me to the brink of suicide.

The Lord intervened, thwarting the evil attack, and ultimately rewarded me with the fulfillment of my righteous desire.

Now, my newfound righteous desire is to witness your success in navigating the "Psalms Path" without enduring the hardships I faced. Having undergone the entire journey, I've become a leading authority on this subject through scripture, prayer, and personal experience. I harbor no regrets; instead, I am grateful for the new life bestowed upon us by our Lord. May our heavenly Father bless you abundantly in all your endeavors.

THE MAKING OF MY RIGHTEOUS DESIRE

I am the son of a remarkable cancer survivor. Back in 2007 my mother, Peggy, confronted a grim diagnosis of stage four non-Hodgkin's lymphoma, with doctors giving her just three months to live. Opting for conventional chemotherapy, she endured a harrowing experience that led to her death in the infusion chair.

The doctors revived her, purged as much of the chemotherapy as possible, and sent her home with little hope. However, my father, Jim, made the decision to take my mother to a small clinic in Mexico. Despite arriving on the brink of death, just a few weeks later, she emerged from the clinic completely free of any signs of disease.

This astonishing recovery stood as the most significant medical miracle we had ever witnessed. Against all odds, my mother continued to live for an additional twelve years, defying the expectations of conventional doctors who initially gave her only twelve weeks.

My father began sharing her remarkable survival story on the internet and included his personal cell phone number on their webpage. However, his success quickly overwhelmed him, leaving him with little time—often only managing to shower once a week.

In December of 2013, my dad invited me to join him in transforming his efforts into a business. Collaboratively, we established the largest online cancer patient advocacy business in the US.

Our work inspired and brought hope to hundreds—if not thousands—of people, encouraging them that survival was possible; and indeed, many of them did survive.

In 2017, my wife and I felt a divine prompting to seek a new purpose, feeling uncertain about our aspirations. Through persistent prayer, we diligently asked God for a God-given desire, nearly every day for about two years. This ultimately led to the revelation of our righteous desire.

Specifically, I felt called to establish our own clinic in Arizona, with the aim of providing the same medical miracles we had witnessed in Mexico.

Interestingly, it became apparent that most individuals were hesitant to seek cancer treatments in Mexico, as they expected the best care to be available in the US. Despite the desire for top-notch healthcare, people reluctantly went to Mexico when they felt they had no other option.

Thus, I relied on the guidance of the Lord to direct me on what steps to take and when to take them, and He faithfully provided the necessary guidance. Despite my limitations, in late November 2019 we opened a natural/alternative cancer clinic in Scottsdale, Arizona. Presently, the clinic is rapidly emerging as a leader in the holistic integrative cancer treatment field.

It stands out as an incredible haven for healing, surpassing the performance of natural cancer clinics in Mexico and the US. Boasting remarkable therapies, exceptional medical expertise, and a staff blessed beyond measure, our clinic has achieved success despite facing substantial challenges.

While I sincerely hope none of you ever require our services, if you or a loved one are seeking hope for surviving cancer, Brio Medical in Scottsdale, Arizona, is the ideal clinic for your needs.

I experienced a rollercoaster of emotions and encountered setbacks, limitations, and heartbreaks that seemed insurmountable. The specter of bankruptcy loomed every two weeks for a staggering two and a half years.

Fretting became a frequent companion, even turning into the lighthearted term "abandon ship moments," where I humorously contemplated whether to

"ABANDON SHIP OR ABANDON HOPE."

In our Lord,
Rusty Roberts

INTRODUCTION

The Psalms Path derives its inspiration from Psalm 37:1-8, authored by King David. It extends a conditional invitation to every child of God, inviting them to co-create righteous desires with the Lord.

These desires are bigger than we think and more than we ask for, and are divinely manifested into our realities, aiming to elevate believers from mere Christians to impactful disciples of Jesus. While being a Christian is admirable, Jesus calls us to be His disciples, lacking nothing and changing their worlds around them.

The Psalms Path stands out as one of the most transformative passages in the Bible. This workbook aims to unveil the genuine significance of these scriptures, drawing from my personal experiences of living out each verse comprehensively. Through constant meditation and ongoing reflection, the Lord communicated with me, providing visions that brought unparalleled clarity to these scriptures. This clarity allows me to share their meanings with you as they pertain to the Psalms Path.

Within the pages of this workbook, you will discover how our Lord grants us righteous desires, the purpose behind these righteous desires, the expectations set for us, what we can anticipate from Him, guidance for daily living, and the remarkable, life-transforming rewards awaiting those who obediently follow the Psalms Path. The Psalms Path is intricately woven within Psalm 37:1-8.

THE PSALMS PATH (PSALM 37:1-8 NKJV)

Psalm 37:1 *Do not fret because of evildoers,*
Nor be envious of the workers of iniquity.
37:2 *For they shall soon be cut down like the grass,*
And wither as the green herb.
37:3 *Trust in the LORD, and do good;*
Dwell in the land, and feed on His faithfulness.
37:4 *Delight yourself also in the LORD,*
And He shall give you the desires of your heart.
37:5 *Commit your way to the LORD,*
Trust also in Him, and He shall bring it to pass.
37:6 *He shall bring forth your righteousness as the light,*
And your justice as the noonday.
37:7 *Rest in the LORD, and wait patiently for Him;*
Do not fret because of him who prospers in his way,
Because of the man who brings wicked schemes to pass.
37:8 *Cease from anger, and forsake wrath; Do not fret—*
it only causes harm.

Chapter 1
Co-Creators with God

We begin with the essence of the Psalms Path, encapsulated in Psalm 37:4-5 (NKJV), *"Delight yourself also in the LORD, and He shall give you the desires of your heart. Commit your way to the LORD, trust also in Him, and He shall bring it to pass."*

These scriptures are conditional, signifying a reciprocal relationship with God where our actions prompt His response. The astounding reality is that the Creator of the universe desires a genuine, loving Father/child relationship with us through His Son, Jesus, as emphasized in verse 4, urging us to "delight in the Lord."

Authenticity is key; our Lord knows our hearts intimately and calls us to a true relationship with Him. When we embrace this connection, we experience the richness of His righteousness and the manifestation of His Spirit's fruits into our spirits: love, joy, peace, patience, kindness, goodness, faithfulness, gentleness, and self-control.

The Psalms Path delves into desires that transcend the mundane; these are not born from our own fleshly inclinations. God does not fulfill desires rooted in self-serving motives, as is made clear in James 4:1-3. Our inherent evil nature is revealed in Isaiah 64:6, as Isaiah renders our best intentions comparable to filthy rags in the eyes of the Lord. Psalm 37:4-5, however, unveils a profound truth—in the intimate Father/child relationship with our heavenly Father, He imparts righteous desires aligned with His purpose for our lives. We come to desire what He desires for us, a truth echoed in Philippians 2:13, affirming that God works within us to fulfill His good purpose.

A noteworthy aspect is the actionable nature of the Psalms Path, presenting an adventure of co-creation with God. Jesus, in John 14:14, explicitly encourages us to ask the Lord for what we want, underscoring our role as co-creators. This invites us to embark on the journey of seeking righteous desires from God by simply asking for them in Jesus' name.

In summary, the Psalms Path was penned by King David, serving as a prophetic message applicable to all of God's children since its inception. It presents a conditional invitation to co-create with the Lord in manifesting righteous desires.

God is orchestrating a transformation within you, lifting you above your inherent capabilities. These righteous desires will be bigger than you think and more than you ask of Him. Rather, your righteous desires stem from the boundless riches of God. This truth is affirmed by Ephesians 3:20 in the scriptures.

God will bring your righteous desires to fruition in your life, despite any external challenges that may arise. The only obstacle that can hinder your righteous desires from manifesting is yourself. In three out of the eight verses that compose the Psalms Path, we are instructed not to fret, as worry poses the greatest threat to your righteous desires.

<u>Your biggest threat is to fret! Do not fret! Psalm 37:8</u>

Fretting entails doubting the word of the Lord. It's crucial to avoid fretting, as it only leads to harm. Instead, trust in the Lord's promise to bring you success. Why question His word when He has assured you of His faithfulness?

God extends this invitation not because you are a good Christian, but for reasons that the final chapter of this book will make clear.

Scriptures:

James 4:1-3 (NIV), *"What causes fights and quarrels among you? Don't they come from your desires that battle within you? You desire but do not have, so you kill. You covet but you cannot get what you want, so you quarrel and fight. You do not have because you do not ask God. When you ask, you do not receive, because you ask with wrong motives, that you may spend what you get on your pleasures."*

Isaiah 64:6 (NIV), *"All of us have become like one who is unclean, and all our righteous acts are like filthy rags."*

Philippians 2:13 (NIV), *"For it is God who works in you to will and to act in order to fulfill his good purpose."*

John 14:14 (NIV), *"You may ask me for anything in my name, and I will do it."*

Ephesians 3:20 (KJV), *"Now unto him that is able to do exceeding abundantly above all that we ask or think, according to the power that worketh in us."*

<u>Prayer:</u> *Gracious heavenly Father, blessed is Your Holy name. Thank You for Jesus, Your Holy Spirit, and Your written Word. I thank You, Lord, for allowing me to be a co-creator of righteous desires for my life. Lord, please give me a righteous desire that is above my ability to make a reality in this world. In Jesus' name I ask, amen.*

———

I recommend persistently seeking a righteous desire from the Lord each day, until you are certain that you have received one. Now, let's delve into the criteria for determining what constitutes a righteous desire.

Chapter 2

5 Criteria for Righteous Desires:
1. You will genuinely desire it (Psalm 37:4).
2. It will bring goodness to your life (1 Thessalonians 5:15).
3. It will contribute positively to all others (1 Thessalonians 5:15).
4. It will glorify God (John 15:8).
5. God will be the one to bring it into reality (Psalm 37:5).

Now we possess a clearer understanding of God's promise to grant us the desires of our hearts. Anticipate that the righteous desire bestowed by God will surpass your own ability to bring it to fruition.

Remember, we are co-creators with the Lord. Revel in your relationship with Him, and God will bestow upon you a righteous desire that exceeds your capabilities.

This truth is affirmed in Ephesians 3:20 (NKJV), which states, *"Now to Him who is able to do exceedingly abundantly above all that we ask or think, according to the power that works in us."*

God, in His glory, surpasses our expectations when we seek righteous things. This underscores why the Bible serves as an instructional guide on how to lead a righteous life in a fallen world.

Remember, your righteous desire will be bigger than you think and more than you ask of God. This is by His design for God the Father's glory.

Session 1 Questions:

1. According to the Psalms Path, what kind of relationship does the Creator of the universe desire with us, and how is it emphasized in verse 4?

   In this genuine Father/child relationship, the child places trust in the Father, believing that the Father has the child's best interests at heart and possesses the ability to bring positive transformations into the child's life. The child will cherish the outcomes without any regrets.

   (Free Writing)

2. What are the five criteria to confirm that you have received a righteous desire from God?
   1. You will genuinely desire it.
   2. It will bring goodness to your life.
   3. It will contribute positively to others.
   4. It will glorify God.
   5. God will be the one to bring it into reality.

   (Free Writing)

3. Why is authenticity highlighted as key in establishing a true relationship with the Lord?

   Authenticity is key; our Lord, who knows our hearts intimately, calls for a true relationship.

   (Free Writing)

4. Describe the conditional nature of Psalm 37:3-5 and the reciprocal relationship it signifies.

   We should fully yield our lives to Him and have faith in Him for the results of our journey.

   (Free Writing)

5. Why does God not fulfill desires rooted in self-serving motives, as mentioned in James 4:1-3?

   James 4:1-3 is written about Christians' fleshly desires causing us to fight, kill, and covet others' lives because we can't get what we want. God does not fulfill these desires rooted in self-serving motives, as is made clear in James 4:1-3. Inherent evil nature, revealed in Isaiah 64:6, renders our best intentions comparable to filthy rags in the eyes of the Lord.

   (Free Writing)

6. According to Jesus' instruction in John 14:14, what is emphasized regarding our role in seeking desires from God?

   The Lord is conveying that when we seek His will in all our endeavors, our prayers will naturally revolve around the fulfillment of righteous desires. In doing so, every prayer request in Jesus' name will be aligned with His holy will, and we should expect that it will be granted.

   (Free Writing)

7. List the fruits of the Spirit mentioned in the Psalms Path that result from embracing a genuine connection with the Lord.

   Love, joy, peace, patience, kindness, generosity, faithfulness, gentleness, and self-control.

   (Free Writing)

8. How does the Psalms Path approach desires, and what distinguishes them from mundane desires?

   The Psalms Path delves into desires that transcend the mundane; these are not born from our own fleshly inclinations. Psalm 37:4 is specifically about righteous desires given to us by God.

   (Free Writing)

9. What truth is unveiled in Psalm 37:4-5 regarding righteous desires and the Father/child relationship?

   The astounding reality is that the Creator of the universe desires a genuine, loving Father/child relationship with us through His Son, Jesus, as emphasized in verse 4 urging us to "delight in the Lord."

   (Free Writing)

10. How does the Psalms Path explain the role of co-creation with God in the context of the Psalms Path?

As children, our duty is to obediently follow our God, recognizing that He comprehends what is optimal for us and can foresee all potential future outcomes in our lives. We are to have confidence that He prioritizes our well-being and is capable of orchestrating the most favorable outcome in this life and the life to come.

(Free Writing)

11. What is the essence of the Psalms Path, as encapsulated in Psalm 37:3-5?

Our heavenly Father is providing His children with the chance to collaboratively bring forth righteous desires through trusting that He will instill them in our hearts and bring them into our realities.

(Free Writing)

Activities List:
1. Actively pray and meditate on the goodness of our Lord, thanking Him for His amazing offer to you to co-create righteous desires that He will manifest into your life.
2. Begin keeping a journal. Take this opportunity to jot down the desires you would harbor for your life if you possessed abilities surpassing your natural capacities.
3. Quote the proceeding scriptures out loud. This is to help you remove any doubts. You must not entertain any doubts of God's promises. Quote Psalm 37:8 out loud ten times each day going forward. Quote 1 Thessalonians 5:16-18 ten times each day going forward.

—

By actively participating in these activities, you can deepen your trust in God's promises, overcome doubt and fretting, and experience the abundant life that comes from surrendering to His will.

Chapter 3
Your Daily Duties

It is your responsibility to <u>delight</u> in the Lord, <u>commit your way</u> to Him, and place your <u>trust in</u> Him.

Your background—whether black, white, or brown—your financial status, wealthy, poor, or somewhere in the middle, your location—whether in a city or the countryside—and even your educational background, do not determine your worthiness of being an elevated disciple of Jesus, living out your righteous desire. It's a gift. God is indifferent to societal standards of beauty, height, or other outward measures. His desire is simply for you to love Him and His Son, Jesus, and to responsibly use the portion of His Spirit which He has graciously given you.

Matthew 16:24 conveys Jesus' message to the disciples, urging them to deny themselves, take up their cross, and follow Him. Likewise, Matthew 11:28-29 encourages embracing Jesus' yoke, promising rest for weary souls, as His yoke is easy and His burden is light.

Becoming an elevated disciple of Jesus is not a solo endeavor. It's about wholeheartedly loving God and His Son, Jesus, allowing them to ignite a divine passion within you. The outcome is a life lived in alignment with your righteous desires guided by God's transformative power, making you an elevated disciple of Jesus, overflowing with His Holy Spirit and impacting the world everywhere you go.

Psalm 37:3-5 (NKJV) states,

> "*Trust* in the Lord and *do good; dwell* in the land, and *feed* on His faithfulness. *Delight* yourself also in the LORD, and He shall give you the desires of your heart. *Commit* your way to the LORD, *trust* also in Him, and He shall bring it to pass."

All seven of these duties are essential for witnessing your righteous desires materialize successfully. These duties are your part of co-creating your righteous desire. As previously mentioned, the Lord desires us to engage in a genuine relationship with Him. This involves taking pleasure in reading His Holy Bible on a daily basis, engaging in daily prayer, and fostering growth in the ways of righteousness.

Matthew 22:37 underscores the importance of loving the Lord with all your heart, soul, and mind. The act of "doing good" is physical acts that display the fruits of the Holy Spirit, as outlined in Galatians 5:22-23, including love, joy, peace, patience, kindness, goodness, faithfulness, gentleness, and self-control.

Philippians 2:13-15 emphasizes God's work within us to fulfill His good purpose, urging us to conduct ourselves without grumbling or arguing, shining as stars in a warped and crooked generation.

The transformative process unfolds as the Lord works in your heart and life, shaping you to resemble His Son, Jesus, leading to a passionate commitment to God and the realization of your righteous desires.

Keep in mind that God will fulfill your righteous desires as you diligently attend to your spiritual responsibilities as expressed in Psalm 37:3-5. These duties are not meant to be overly burdensome, but rather to bring you joy and make your life easier. By faithfully carrying out these spiritual duties, you'll find peace and avoid fretting as you patiently await the Lord to bring your righteous desires to fruition.

In conclusion, the essence of the "Your Daily Duties" chapter is to provide you with actionable steps that redirect the focus of your life from yourself to our Lord Jesus. When you willingly relinquish the throne of your personal universe and invite Jesus to reign, your life will take off like a rocket. This concept is beautifully encapsulated in Proverbs 16:3 (NASB), emphasizing your role as a co-creator with the Lord: *"Commit your works to the LORD, and your plans will be established."* Your journey along the Psalms Path can be simplified when you stop thinking about *you* all the time and center your life around Jesus. The duties God has laid out for you are the actions that will transform you into the person He will entrust with an amazing righteous desire.

Scriptures:

Matthew 22:37 (NIV), *"Jesus replied: 'Love the Lord your God with all your heart and with all your soul and with all your mind.'"*

Psalm 37:4-5 (NKJV), *"Delight yourself also in the LORD, and He shall give you the desires of your heart. Commit your way to the LORD, trust also in Him, and He shall bring it to pass."*

Galatians 5:22 (NIV), *"But the fruit of the Spirit is love, joy, peace, forbearance, kindness, goodness, faithfulness, gentleness and self-control. Against such things, there is no law."*

Philippians 2:13 (NIV), *"For it is God who works in you to will and to act in order to fulfill his good purpose."*

Ephesians 3:20 (NIV), *"Now to him who is able to do immeasurably more than all we ask or imagine, according to his power that is at work within us."*

Proverbs 3:5-6 (NIV), *"Trust in the LORD with all your heart and lean not on your own understanding; in all your ways submit to him, and he will make your paths straight."*

Psalm 118:8 (NIV), *"It is better to take refuge in the LORD than to trust in humans."*

Hebrews 11:6 (NIV), *"And without faith it is impossible to please God, because anyone who comes to him must believe that he exists and that he rewards those who earnestly seek him."*

2 Corinthians 5:7 (NIV), *"We live by faith, not by sight."*

Proverbs 16:3 (KJV), *"Commit thy works unto the LORD, and thy thoughts shall be established."*

Activities List:
1. **Trust-building exercises:** Spend time reflecting on moments in your life where you have seen God's faithfulness. Journal about these experiences and meditate on how they demonstrate God's trustworthiness. Pray for an increase in trust in the Lord, and ask Him to help you rely more fully on His promises.
2. **Acts of kindness:** Purposefully seek opportunities to do good for others. Volunteer at your church, help a neighbor in need, or simply show kindness and compassion to those around you. By doing good, you are actively demonstrating your trust in the Lord's command to "do good" as stated in the passage. These acts give you the opportunity to display the Lord's fruits of the Spirit.
3. **Mindfulness in God's presence:** Allocate time daily to immerse yourself in the presence of the Lord through prayer, meditation, and scripture reading. This practice will shift your focus away from yourself and onto the Lord Jesus. Actively prioritizing Jesus as the center of your life is crucial for the Lord to bring your righteous desire to pass. I suggest reading a chapter of the Gospels every day.

4. **Practice gratitude:** Cultivate a daily practice of expressing gratitude verbally, where you intentionally recognize and thank God for His faithfulness and provision in your life. Keep a gratitude journal where you write down specific things you are thankful for each day. This practice will help you cultivate a heart of gratitude and delight in the Lord's goodness. Every day, express gratitude to God for His priceless gifts: Jesus, the Holy Spirit, and the Holy Bible. These divine offerings make life meaningful and surpass any personal challenges you may encounter.
5. **Commitment to God's ways:** Read Proverbs 3:5-6 daily, as you need to actively acknowledge the Lord in all your ways. This means you think about what God would want in every situation in your current life. Pray to God that He will reveal His desires and plans to you. Bear in mind that God may not disclose the entire picture all at once. Anticipate that He will unveil only what is necessary for you to take the next step successfully.

—

By actively engaging in these activities, you are fulfilling the call to find joy in the Lord, dedicate your path to Him, and place your trust in Him, as outlined in Psalm 37:3-5.

Bonus Scriptures:

Matthew 16:25 (NIV), *"For whoever wants to save their life will lose it, but whoever loses their life for me will find it."*

Moving to Matthew 11:28-29, Jesus extends an invitation to those weary of the world's burdens. He assures His followers that a life dedicated to God the Father is inherently lighter than one focused solely on personal desires.

Chapter 4
Satan Will Try to Kill Your Righteous Desire

Psalm 37:6 (NKJV) says, *"He shall bring forth your righteousness as the light, and your justice as the noonday."* As you walk the Psalms Path, you will be transformed to reflect Jesus' nature. People are going to see the changes in you as a light brightens a dark room. People will see it, and Satan will see it. The devil and his horde of demons will be able to see your light shining from a far-off distance. The Lord gave me a vision which brings clarity.

The Vision:

Upon a mountainous outcrop overlooking Los Angeles, a horde of evil spirits observed the city engulfed in darkness. These spirits existed in perpetual darkness. In the moonlit city, devoid of typical lights, beams of light shot upward like spotlights in different places throughout the city. The malevolent spirits keenly watched these lights. Suddenly, a new light emerged on the left side of the city. The malevolent spirit in charge commanded the three immediate evil spirits on his left, "Go kill it."

This vision served as a warning—Satan and his fallen angels can discern the birth of our righteous desires, recognizing the threat it poses to them. Consequently, they vigorously oppose the realization of your righteous desires, deploying various attacks as noted in Psalm 37:1-8.

1. When faced with various types of evil attacks, refrain from fretting about them.
2. Even if those around you experience prosperity as you encounter obstacles, resist the urge to fret.
3. Refrain from fretting about your worthiness, readiness, or God's ability to see you through challenging situations.

Actively resist the urge to doubt! Read 1 Thessalonians 5:16-18 (NIV) out loud daily: *"Rejoice always, pray continually, give thanks in all circumstances; for this is God's will for you in Christ Jesus."*

It's essential to recognize that achieving this is beyond your own capabilities, skills, or education. Despite your limitations, the Lord will bring about its fulfillment in His perfect timing, not according to your schedule.

Therefore, as you commit to turning your righteous desire into reality, expect skepticism and opposition even from friends and family, who may view your pursuit as impractical.

Your journey may be perilous, akin to the Israelites facing the Red Sea while pursued by the Egyptian army. Despite apparent disaster, the Lord orchestrates miracles at the appointed time.

Prepare for naysayers and challenges; the Lord promises vindication at the right moment (Psalm 37:6 (NIV), *"Your vindication like the noonday."*). This is the moment when the shadows of doubt are at their smallest, as your righteous desire becomes a solid reality in this world, and all those doubters who didn't believe it was possible will have witnessed you achieve the seemingly impossible.

Remember, it was the Lord who brought you through everything. Give thanks to Him. Proverbs 27:1 (NKJV), *"Do not boast about tomorrow, for you do not know what a day may bring forth."*

Success is not guaranteed by earthly promises, but by God's assurance. Embrace the hardships, understanding that your success is a unique journey between you and the Lord.

Walking the Psalms Path may instill fear, but the ultimate rewards make it worthwhile. Do not fret; it only causes harm— Psalm 37:8.

Remaining focused on the ultimate goal, as emphasized in Psalm 37:6 where your justice shines like the noonday, leads to divine rewards. Trust that—at the right time—the Lord will actualize your righteous desire.

It's essential to acknowledge that your own abilities, skills, or education won't be the driving force; the Lord will orchestrate it on your behalf.

Note*

A moment of reflection is necessary. Neither I nor anyone on this earth can guarantee your success in obtaining your righteous desires as you walk the Psalms Path.

This journey is uniquely yours, shared only with the Lord.

Various challenges, each unique, will inevitably arise, but take comfort in the assurance of God's promise of your success. Drawing from my own experience, stepping onto the Psalms Path initially felt daunting, as I wasn't entirely prepared.

However, despite the uncertainties, the journey proved to be incredibly rewarding and worthwhile.

Chapter 5
Reality Check

It's time to face a sobering truth: as previously stated, your righteous desire cannot be achieved through your own efforts alone. It is not something that can be earned or guaranteed by anyone in this world; rather, it is a reward bestowed on you by the Lord.

Your righteous desire is not a debt owed to you by God, and it should never take precedence over your relationship with Him.

It's crucial to avoid elevating your righteous desire to the status of an idol, a mistake I once made. Scripture offers clear guidance on the godly priorities we should uphold in our life's journey.

Luke 14:26 teaches us to prioritize our relationship with God above all else, emphasizing a deep love for Him that surpasses any other attachment. It's important to understand that when the scripture uses the term "hate," it actually conveys the concept of loving less. This perspective ensures that the righteous desire within you is not idolized, but seen within the context of your profound love for the Lord.

Guard against making your righteous desire an idol, as the Lord may withhold its realization if it threatens to overshadow your relationship with Him. Satan seeks to undermine your righteous desires by any means, and prioritizing them over your connection with God can lead you to doubt God's Word, thereby playing right into Satan's hands.

In contrast, Proverbs 3:5-6 offers an uplifting perspective, urging us to place our complete trust in the Lord. By acknowledging Him in all our ways, we invite His divine guidance into our lives.

Important Note:

Successfully manifesting your righteous desires requires confronting any hidden sins in your life. This revelation may serve as a pivotal moment of truth, especially for those harboring significant sins.

Despite the discomfort, it's crucial to acknowledge that the Lord mandates the removal of hidden sins. Proverbs 28:13 (NKJV) underscores this truth: *"He who covers his sins will not prosper, but whoever confesses and forsakes them will have mercy."*

It's important to note that while seeking mercy is paramount, it may not guarantee forgiveness from those we have wronged. Although challenging, it's a necessary step on the path to fulfilling our righteous desires as God's children.

This encapsulates the essence of the Psalms Path, and I trust the message is now unmistakably clear and deeply inspiring.

<u>What goes on in Vegas does not stay in Vegas.</u>

Scriptures:

Luke 14:26 (KJV) says, *"If any man come to me, and hate not his father, and mother, and wife, and children, and brethren, and sisters, yea, and his own life also, he cannot be my disciple."*

Proverbs 3:5-6 (NKJV) says, *"Trust in the LORD with all your heart, and lean not on your own understanding; in all your ways acknowledge Him, and He shall direct your paths."*

Proverbs 28:13 (NKJV) says, *"He who covers his sins will not prosper, but whoever confesses and forsakes them will have mercy."*

Chapter 6
Circumstances That Could Occur When Walking the Psalms Path

1. An evil act will most likely occur. Don't fret about it. (Psalm 37:1, 7)
2. People in your life may start prospering while you are trying to overcome obstacles. Don't fret about it. (Psalm 37:7)
3. Your righteous desire will likely require more time than anticipated to solidify into reality. Don't fret about it. (Psalm 37:7)
4. The Psalms Path is designed by God to foster your spiritual growth and ultimately reward you with a fulfilling life aligned with your dreams. Be excited about it. (Psalm 37:3-5)
5. You absolutely should not fret (the acts of worry and anxiety). (Psalm 37:1, 7-8)
6. You will succeed regardless of all the challenges you will face. Stay convicted of it. (Psalm 37:5-6)
7. Your righteous desire becoming a reality is not more important than your relationship with God. He doesn't owe it to you. Don't let your righteous desire become your idol. (Luke 14:26)

Session 2 Questions:

1. What does Psalm 37:6 say about the manifestation of righteousness and justice?

   Psalm 37:6 (NKJV) says, *"He shall bring forth your righteousness as the light, and your justice as the noonday."* As you walk the Psalms Path, you will be transformed to better reflect Jesus' nature. People are going to see the changes in you as a light brightens a dark room. People will see it, and Satan will see it.

   (Free Writing)

2. How does walking the Psalms Path lead to a transformation reflecting Jesus' nature?

   Psalm 37:3-5 emphasizes the necessity of wholeheartedly surrendering our hearts to God the Father. This entails relinquishing our sinful ways and genuinely striving to lead a righteous life, mirroring the example set by Jesus. In Psalm 37:5, the message is to entrust every aspect of our lives to God the Father and have faith that He has our best interests at heart.

   (Free Writing)

3. In what way is the analogy of light brightening a dark room used to illustrate the changes people will see in you?

   Having a guiding light helps us navigate our surroundings without stumbling or getting hurt. When we live according to the Lord's guidance in a fallen world, we find success in all our endeavors, witness the fulfillment of our prayers at the right time, and receive every righteous desire bestowed by God.

   (Free Writing)

4. According to the Psalms Path, who will be able to perceive the transformation as your light shines?

   Those in our circle—friends, family, co-workers, employers—will witness the evident blessings in every facet of our life. Even Satan and his malevolent forces will observe that you are aligning with God's plan, attempting to instigate doubt about the outcomes. If Satan succeeds, it may lead to questioning God's Word, potentially hindering the realization of your righteous desires.

   (Free Writing)

5. What role does Satan play in the context of your journey on the Psalms Path?

   Satan's sole purpose is to steal, kill, and destroy your righteous desires. However, his presence presents us with the chance to entrust the outcomes to our Lord without succumbing to anxiety. In doing so, we actively participate as co-creators of the righteous desires bestowed upon us by God the Father.

   (Free Writing)

6. How is the vision described in the Psalms Path significant in understanding the visibility of your light?

   The vision provides clarity that Psalm 37:6 goes beyond mere eloquence; it serves as a caution that Satan will undoubtedly attempt to hinder you because you are destined to be a blessing to those around you. It advises against succumbing to anxiety in the face of Satan's attacks.

   (Free Writing)

Activities List:

1. **Daily Reflection:** Set aside time each day to reflect on any potential evil acts which could be brewing in your life. For instance, if you're moving, you may want to consider taking out insurance on your household goods and personally moving your keepsakes. Do not ignore red flags. Practice releasing worry and anxiety about these situations, trusting in God's sovereignty and protection. (Psalm 37:1, 7; Luke 12:25-26)
2. **Gratitude Journaling:** Keep a gratitude journal where you regularly write down blessings in your life, even when others seem to be prospering while you face obstacles. Cultivate a heart of gratitude and contentment regardless of external circumstances. (Psalm 37:7; Philippians 4:11-12)
3. **Patience Practice:** Engage in activities that require patience and perseverance, recognizing that your righteous desires may take longer than expected to materialize. Practice trusting in God's timing and remaining steadfast in faith. (Psalm 37:7; Hebrews 10:36)
4. **Vision Board Creation:** Create a vision board or visualization exercises that depict your dreams and desires aligned with God's will for your life. Use Psalm 37:3-5 as inspiration, trusting that God will fulfill His promises as you commit your ways to Him. (Psalm 37:3-5; Habakkuk 2:2-3)
5. **Anxiety Management:** Practice techniques to manage and alleviate worry and anxiety, such as deep breathing, prayer, and mindfulness. Remember that fretting is not productive and can hinder your spiritual growth. (Psalm 37:1, 7-8; Matthew 6:25-34)

6. **Confidence Building:** Engage in activities that build confidence and conviction in God's promises, knowing that you will succeed despite challenges. Reflect on past victories and God's faithfulness to bolster your faith. (Psalm 37:5-6; Romans 8:37)
7. **Priority Evaluation:** Reflect on your priorities and ensure that your righteous desires do not overshadow your relationship with God. Practice surrendering your desires to God's will and guarding against idolizing them. (Luke 14:26; Matthew 6:33)

Chapter 7
Psalms Path Verses 1, 2, 3, 6, 7, 8 with Supporting Scriptures

Psalm 37:1

Psalm 37:1 (NKJV) advises, *"Do not fret because of evildoers, nor be envious of the workers of iniquity."* As I mentioned earlier regarding the devil's schemes, anticipate potential evil attacks—perhaps more than one. Stay vigilant and be on guard, paying attention to any red flags and not ignoring them.

However, the Lord explicitly instructs us not to fret, avoiding worry or anxiety in the face of such attacks. The Lord desires our preparedness, so that when these assaults occur, we anticipate them, act in accordance with His will, and mitigate their impact on our lives.

In 1 Thessalonians 5:16-18 (NIV), we are reminded to *"Rejoice always, pray continually, give thanks in all circumstances; for this is God's will for you in Christ Jesus."* Spiritual awareness and preparation are crucial, ensuring we don't perceive God's abandonment but recognize these challenges as part of the Psalms Path. Stay resilient, knowing your righteous desire is on its way.

Furthermore, the Lord outlines the fate of those engaging in evil deeds or working in sinful ways in Psalm 37:2 (KJV), stating, *"For they shall soon be cut down like the grass, and wither as the green herb."* This signifies that the Lord will address their actions on your behalf, relieving you of the need to worry.

Romans 12:19-21 reinforces this perspective, urging believers not to seek vengeance but to leave room for the Lord's retribution.

It emphasizes responding to enemies with kindness, understanding that overcoming evil is achieved through acts of goodness.

The Lord encourages us to refrain from plotting revenge, and instead steer our hearts toward thoughts of His goodness.

Scripture:

Psalm 37:2 (KJV), *"For they shall soon be cut down like the grass, and wither as the green herb."*

Romans 12:19-21 (KJV), *"Dearly beloved, avenge not yourselves, but rather give place unto wrath: for it is written, Vengeance is mine; I will repay, saith the Lord.*

Therefore if thine enemy hunger, feed him; if he thirst, give him drink: for in so doing thou shalt heap coals of fire on his head. Be not overcome of evil, but overcome evil with good."

Psalm 37:3 (NKJV), *"Trust in the LORD, and do good; dwell in the land, and feed on His faithfulness."* This scripture provides specific guidance on how to live daily as we navigate the Psalms Path.

―

Let's explore the significance of Psalm 37:3, unpacking its profound meaning.

Trusting, synonymous with *believing*, entails placing confidence in the unwavering belief that God is watching over and ready to assist and protect. Wholeheartedly embracing His plans requires unshakeable trust.

This trust isn't unfounded; it's firmly anchored in the faithfulness and goodness of our God. As we delve into the scriptures, acquaint ourselves with God's promises, and witness His unwavering faithfulness to the Israelites, Abraham, and each of us, our comprehension of God's character will deepen.

Proverbs 3:5-6 complements this, urging us to trust in the Lord with all our hearts and lean not on our own understanding, promising that as we submit to Him, He will make our paths straight.

Four Reasons to Trust in God:
1. He knows better than we do.
2. All things are possible with God.
3. He is worthy of our trust.
4. He knows what He is doing.

Continuing with the verse, "Do good," it extends beyond moments of ease; it holds equal significance during times of hardship. Experiencing obstacles in life can foster empathy for others. It's crucial to recognize that the Lord values not only our spiritual growth but also our expression of kindness to His creation, especially our fellow believers.

Titus 3:14 emphasizes the importance of dedicating ourselves to good works, aiding urgent needs, and avoiding unfruitfulness.

Now that you've gained a clearer understanding of what God conveys with "Dwell in the land," let's explore the rest of the scripture: "...and feed on His faithfulness."

To grasp this concept, consider Jeremiah 15:16, which likens the consumption of God's words to the joy and rejoicing of the heart.

Just as food nourishes every cell in our bodies, regularly immersing ourselves in God's scripture feeds our spirits.

Psalm 37:3, with its call to dwell and feed, becomes essential for you as a co-creator of righteous desires. However, a word of caution: desiring the outcome of a righteous desire demands spiritual readiness.

I urge you not to seek a righteous desire if you're not willing to become spiritually prepared. I speak from personal experience, having lived in fear for two and a half years after receiving an unprepared-for righteous desire.

Take the time provided by God to mature spiritually, ensuring that when your righteous desire materializes, it's initially embraced as a blessing.

Chapter 8
Don't Waste the Wait

In Psalm 37, God emphasizes three times not to fret (verses one, seven, and eight). It's crucial to understand that God won't prevent Satan from attempting to thwart your righteous desire.

Remember, as co-creators with the Lord, we receive clear instructions on how to live daily and what to anticipate on this remarkable path known as the Psalms Path.

Scripture:

Psalm 37:3 (NKJV), *"Trust in the LORD, and do good; dwell in the land, and feed on His faithfulness."*

Proverbs 3:5-6 (NIV), *"Trust in the Lord with all your heart and lean not on your own understanding; in all your ways submit to Him, and He will make your paths straight."*

Titus 3:14 (RSV), *"And let our people learn to apply themselves to good deeds, so as to help cases of urgent need, and not to be unfruitful."*

Galatians 5:16 (KJV), *"This I say then, Walk in the Spirit, and ye shall not fulfill the lust of the flesh."*

Deuteronomy 6:7 (NIV), *"Impress them on your children. Talk about them when you sit at home and when you walk along the road, when you lie down and when you get up."*

Luke 10:27 (KJV), *"And He answering said, Thou shalt love the Lord thy God with all thy heart, and with all thy soul, and with all thy strength, and with all thy mind; and thy neighbor as thyself."*

Romans 6:4 (AKJV), *"Therefore we are buried with him by baptism into death: that like as Christ was raised up from the dead by the glory of the Father, even so we also should walk in newness of life."*

Jeremiah 15:16 (KJV), *"Thy words were found, and I did eat them; and thy word was unto me the joy and rejoicing of mine heart: for I am called by thy name, O LORD God of hosts."*

—

Psalm 37:7 How long will it take to witness success? According to Psalm 37:7 (NKJV), the Lord advises us to exercise patience, emphasizing that the manifestation of our righteous desires may take longer than anticipated. The scripture encourages us to *"Rest in the LORD, and wait patiently for Him; do not fret because of him who prospers in his way, because of the man who brings wicked schemes to pass."* This verse serves as both a timeline and a cautionary note against impatience, as Satan may exploit it to make us stumble or give up. In other words, it is the act of fretting. Do not fret.

It warns us not to be anxious about the timing and outcomes while waiting for our righteous desires to materialize.

In this waiting period, we may observe others around us prospering while we endure challenges. However, the scripture reassures us not to fret or feel abandoned by God.

Instead, we are encouraged to stay focused, rejoice, pray, and give thanks as we witness the unfolding of events, recognizing them as part of the Psalms Path.

Even when others seem to succeed, take heart, knowing that the Lord's will cannot be thwarted by external forces, except by our own actions if we deviate from His instructions as co-creators of our righteous desires.

Throughout this journey, the Lord provides scriptures to nourish our spirits and maintain a joyful spirit during the waiting period. These scriptures guide us on how God works in our lives, emphasizing the importance of faith.

Hebrews 11:1 defines faith as confidence in what we hope for and assurance about what we do not see. James 1:2-4 instructs us to consider trials as opportunities for faith to produce perseverance, leading to maturity.

It's essential to believe in the Lord and expect twists and turns as we walk the Psalms Path. The path requires faith, trust, and acceptance of God's ways, which may differ from our own.

Ecclesiastes 7:13 encourages accepting the way God does things, and Isaiah 55:8-9 emphasizes the distinction between God's thoughts and ours.

Amidst the process of the Psalms Path, the scripture advises against fretting and encourages prayer, supplication, and thanksgiving. Philippians 4:6-7 assures us that the peace of God, surpassing understanding, will guard our hearts and minds through Christ Jesus.

Additional verses, including Matthew 21:22, Mark 11:22, and Mark 9:23, underscore the power of faith in prayer and belief.

Psalm 37:8 The final scripture in the Psalms Path, Psalm 37:8 (NKJV), advises, *"Cease from anger, and forsake wrath; do not fret—it only causes harm."* This scripture highlights that the Psalms Path may lead to moments of anger if we lose focus and start fretting.

In conclusion, the Psalms Path is a conditional scripture requiring faith as a crucial condition for success. John 15:4 stresses the importance of abiding in the Lord, comparing it to a branch bearing fruit when connected to the vine.

Scriptures:

Psalm 37:7 (NKJV), *"Rest in the LORD, and wait patiently for Him; do not fret because of him who prospers in his way, because of the man who brings wicked schemes to pass."*

Isaiah 14:27 (NKJV), *"For the LORD of hosts has purposed, and who will annul it? His hand is stretched out, and who will turn it back?"*

Hebrews 11:1 (NIV), *"Now faith is confidence in what we hope for and assurance about what we do not see."*

James 1:2-4 (NIV), *"Consider it pure joy, my brothers and sisters, whenever you face trials of many kinds, because you know that the testing of your faith produces perseverance. Let perseverance finish its work so that you may be mature and complete, not lacking anything."*

Ecclesiastes 7:13 (NLT), *"Accept the way God does things, for who can straighten what He has made crooked?"*

Isaiah 55:8-9 (NIV), *"'For my thoughts are not your thoughts, neither are your ways my ways,' declares the Lord. 'As the heavens are higher than the earth, so are my ways higher than your ways and my thoughts than your thoughts.'"*

Philippians 4:6-7 (NKJV), *"Be anxious for nothing, but in everything by prayer and supplication, with thanksgiving, let your requests be made known to God; and the peace of God, which surpasses all understanding, will guard your hearts and minds through Christ Jesus."*

Matthew 21:22 (NIV), *"If you believe, you will receive whatever you ask for in prayer."*

Mark 11:22 (NIV), *"'Have faith in God,' Jesus answered. 'Truly I tell you, if anyone says to this mountain, "Go, throw yourself into the sea," and does not doubt in their heart but believes that what they say will happen, it will be done for them. Therefore I tell you, whatever you ask for in prayer, believe that you have received it, and it will be yours."*

Mark 9:23 (NIV), *"Everything is possible for one who believes."*

John 15:4 (NKJV), *"Abide in Me, and I in you. As the branch cannot bear fruit of itself, unless it abides in the vine, neither can you, unless you abide in Me."*

Activities List:

1. **Rest and Patience:** Take time each day to ponder the magnificence of Jesus as God in human form—the Almighty Creator who humbled Himself to dwell among us. Reflect on His selfless service, culminating in the ultimate sacrifice of His life for our eternal salvation. This practice is intended to shift your focus away from yourself and onto the one who truly deserves it, Jesus. As you do so, expect to find rest and cultivate greater patience in your life.
2. **Reflection and Trust:** Reflect on Isaiah 14:27 and meditate on the assurance that God's purposes cannot be annulled. Trust in His sovereignty and the unchanging nature of His plans.
3. **Faith-Building Exercises:** Engage in activities that strengthen your faith, such as studying Hebrews 11:1. Reflect on instances in your life where you have seen God's faithfulness despite not seeing immediate results.
4. **Joy in Trials:** Follow the exhortation in James 1:2-4 by considering trials as opportunities for growth. Practice finding joy in the midst of challenges, knowing that perseverance produces maturity and completeness in your faith.
5. **Acceptance of God's Ways:** Reflect on Ecclesiastes 7:13 and Isaiah 55:8-9. Accept that God's ways are

higher than our ways and His thoughts higher than our thoughts. Surrender the need for understanding and trust in His wisdom and sovereignty.
6. **Prayer and Thanksgiving:** Practice the principles outlined in Philippians 4:6-7. Bring your requests to God through prayer, with thanksgiving, and trust in His peace to guard your heart and mind.
7. **Belief in Prayer:** Embrace the promises of prayer found in Matthew 21:22 and Mark 11:22. Believe that whatever you ask for in prayer, believing, you will receive. Trust in God's power to move mountains and bring about what you ask for.
8. **Faith in Possibility:** Meditate on Mark 9:23 and John 15:4. Remember that with God, all things are possible for those who believe. Abide in Him, remaining connected to the source of life and bearing fruit in accordance with His will.

Three ways to overcome life's obstacles that might cause fretting:

1. **Accept Obstacles:** Recognize that obstacles are inherent in the Psalms Path. Setbacks and challenges are to be expected, and being co-creators of righteous desires involves facing various obstacles. Isaiah 55:8-9 emphasizes the difference between God's ways and our ways, while James 1:2-4 encourages joy in facing trials for the sake of spiritual maturity.
2. **Follow God's Commands:** Acknowledge your human reactions to obstacles, but respond with a calm spirit of obedience to the Lord's commands. The objective is to journey through the Psalms Path, ultimately attaining your righteous desire while achieving spiritual maturity and lacking nothing, as outlined in James 1:2-4.
3. **Wait for Divine Intervention:** Remember that righteous desires can only become realities through God's

intervention. Trust that God will bring it to pass at the right time, as stated in Isaiah 60:22 (NKJV), *"I, the LORD, will hasten it in its time."*

Scriptures:

Psalm 37:8 (NKJV), *"Cease from anger, and forsake wrath; do not fret—it only causes harm."*

Ephesians 4:31-32 (KJV), *"Let all bitterness, and wrath, and anger, and clamour, and evil speaking, be put away from you, with all malice: and be ye kind one to another, tenderhearted, forgiving one another, even as God for Christ's sake hath forgiven you."*

Isaiah 55:8-9 (NIV), *"'For my thoughts are not your thoughts, neither are your ways my ways,' declares the Lord. 'As the heavens are higher than the earth, so are my ways higher than your ways and my thoughts than your thoughts.'"*

James 1:2-4 (NIV), *"Consider it pure joy, my brothers and sisters, whenever you face trials of many kinds, because you know that the testing of your faith produces perseverance. Let perseverance finish its work so that you may be mature and complete, not lacking anything."*

James 1:2-4 (NKJV), *"My brethren, count it all joy when you fall into various trials, knowing that the testing of your faith produces patience. But let patience have its perfect work, that you may be perfect and complete, lacking nothing."*

Isaiah 60:22 (NKJV), *"I, the LORD, will hasten it in its time."*

Activities List:

1. **Anger Management:** Practice ceasing from anger and forsaking wrath, as instructed in Psalm 37:8. Engage in activities such as deep breathing exercises, journaling, or seeking guidance from a trusted mentor to manage feelings of anger and frustration. Reach out to us.
2. **Kindness Practice:** Implement the principles of Ephesians 4:29-32 by intentionally cultivating kindness and compassion towards others. Look for opportunities to speak words of encouragement and build others up, while letting go of bitterness and malice.
3. **Reflection on God's Ways:** Reflect on Isaiah 55:8-9 and meditate on the profound truth that God's thoughts and ways are higher than ours. Spend time in prayer seeking to align your thoughts and actions with God's will, surrendering your own understanding to His wisdom.
4. **Joy in Trials:** Embrace the exhortation in James 1:2-4 to consider it pure joy when facing trials of various kinds. Practice shifting your perspective to view challenges as opportunities for growth and refinement of your faith. Engage in activities such as journaling or prayer to cultivate joy and perseverance amidst trials.
5. **Patience Building:** Follow the guidance of James 1:2-4 in allowing patience to have its perfect work in your life. Practice patience in daily situations, trusting that God's timing is perfect and that He will hasten His plans in due time, as affirmed in Isaiah 60:22.

Chapter 9
Why Would the Lord Allow Us to Co-Create Righteous Desires?

Intriguingly, God grants us the privilege of co-creating righteous desires alongside Him, using them as incentives (bait) for His children to align their aspirations with His divine will. While some might find it unsettling to consider God's use of "bait," it's essential to recall Matthew 4:19 (KJV), where Jesus says, *"And He saith unto them, Follow me, and I will make you fishers of men."* Just as fishermen employ the appropriate bait to catch fish, God employs these desires to draw us closer to His intended path for our lives.

<u>This gives us a new perspective on the term "fishers of men."</u>

The question we must ask ourselves in conclusion is: What is God's intended path for each of our lives? We discover this answer in Matthew 28:19-20 (NKJV), *"'Go therefore and make disciples of all the nations, baptizing them in the name of the Father and the Son and the Holy Spirit, teaching them to observe all things all that I have commanded you; and lo, I am with you always, even to the end of the age.' Amen."*

Jesus expressly summons us to become His disciples, and our foremost mission as disciples is to disciple everyone we encounter.

The fundamental role of a disciple is to learn and gain wisdom from the teacher. Disciples are meant to enhance their comprehension and mirror their teacher's actions. As followers of Jesus, we are tasked with emulating His deeds and embodying His teachings.

John 14:12-14 (KJV), *"Verily, verily, I say unto you, He that believeth on me, the works that I do shall he do also; and greater works than these shall he do; because I go unto my Father. And whatsoever ye shall ask in my name, that will I do, that the Father may be glorified in the Son. If ye shall ask anything in my name, I will do it."*

It's crucial to recognize that as true disciples of Jesus, we are taught to seek only righteous things. Consequently, God will never deny our requests made in accordance with His will. In Jesus' name, we will receive everything we ask for.

Jesus' disciples are called to perform extraordinary acts such as casting out demons, prophesying, healing the sick, restoring sight to the blind, enabling the lame to walk, and even raising the dead. Yet how many of God's children within the global church can honestly claim to have performed these miracles, myself included? As I reflect, I acknowledge that I have not yet witnessed or participated in such extraordinary acts. However, I recognize the profound significance behind the Lord's desire for us to engage in these miraculous deeds.

It's imperative that we prioritize loving God above ourselves. Consider what extraordinary feats the Lord could accomplish through us if we relinquished any desire for personal glory. Let's engage in honest introspection. While recognition for remarkable deeds is certainly gratifying, true fulfillment lies in selflessly serving God's will and allowing His glory to shine through us without seeking recognition for ourselves.

It's possible that our pride may indeed hinder us from fully embracing the miraculous work the Lord intends for us to do. When we prioritize ourselves over God and others, our focus shifts away from selfless service and toward self-gratification. This self-centered mindset can impede our ability to wholeheartedly devote ourselves to God's will and to love others as we love ourselves. Therefore, it's crucial for us to continually examine our hearts and strive to cultivate a spirit of humility and selflessness, enabling us to more effectively serve the Lord and those around us.

Isaiah 42:8 (KJV), *"I am the LORD: that is my name: and my glory will I not give to another."*

Indeed, it is time for us to wholeheartedly surrender our lives to our Lord and King. When we surrender our will to His, we open ourselves up to experiencing the most extraordinary and fulfilling lives imaginable.

In surrendering to Him, we find true purpose, peace, and joy. Our lives become a testimony to His grace and power, and we embark on a journey filled with His abundant blessings and divine guidance. Surrendering to our Lord and King transforms our existence into something truly remarkable, far beyond what we could ever envision or achieve on our own.

In conclusion, the Lord grants us righteous desires that are bigger than we think and more than we ask of Him. Through these desires, God lifts us up to shine as beacons of light in the world. This elevation transforms us from mere Christians into disciples of Jesus. While being Christians is admirable, it's disciples who have the power to truly impact and change the world. As disciples, we are called to embody the teachings of Jesus and actively engage in spreading His message of love, compassion, and redemption to all corners of the earth.

Chapter 10
Concluding Questions and Answers

1. What is the essence of the Psalms Path, as encapsulated in Psalm 37:3-5?

   Our heavenly Father is providing His children with the chance to collaboratively bring forth righteous desires through trusting that He will instill them in our hearts. He is interested in our well-being and is capable of orchestrating the most favorable outcome in this life and the life to come.

   (Free Writing)

2. According to Jesus' instruction in John 14:14, what is emphasized regarding our role in seeking desires from God?

   The Lord is conveying that when we seek His will in all our endeavors, our prayers will naturally revolve around the fulfillment of righteous desires. In doing so, every prayer request aligned with His holy will will be granted.

   (Free Writing)

3. What is the central scripture of the Psalms Path, and what does it emphasize about the relationship with God? Psalm 37:3-5 are the central scriptures, as they emphasize that we will co-create our righteous desires with God.

(Free Writing)

4. Explain the concept of "delighting in the Lord" as mentioned in Psalm 37:4 and its significance in the journey of faith.

Delighting in the Lord is enjoying a true Father/child relationship with Him. We must wholeheartedly give our lives over to our Lord and trust that He will fulfill His promises to us.

(Free Writing)

5. Why does the Psalms Path distinguish between desires originating from the flesh and righteous desires? Provide supporting scriptures.

Fleshly desires cause wars and fights among us. James 4:1-3. Righteous desires are good for us, good for many other people, they glorify God, and we can't create them on our own. 1 Thessalonians 5:15, Psalm 37:5, John 15:7-8.

(Free Writing)

6. In what ways does the Psalms Path encourage believers to be co-creators with God in realizing their desires?

   In Psalm 37:4, the Lord is telling us that we will want it. That is the definition of desire.

   (Free Writing)

7. Share the prayer presented in the Psalms Path. What key elements does it include, and what is the underlying theme?

   Gracious heavenly Father. (Greeting)
   Thank You for Jesus, the Holy Spirit, and Your Bible. (Gratitude)
   Thank You, Lord, for allowing me to be a co-creator of righteous desires for my life. (Gratitude)
   Please give me a righteous desire that is above my ability to make into a reality in my world. In Jesus' name, amen. (The Ask)

   (Free Writing)

8. Revisit the "Daily Duties" section. Why are these duties considered essential for the manifestation of righteous desires?

   The daily duties involve striving to be a faithful child who seeks to please our heavenly Father by dedicating our entire life to Him and entrusting Him with every aspect of our lives. When we do this, He will give us whatever we desire. John 15:7.

   (Free Writing)

9. Summarize the message conveyed in Matthew 16:24 and Matthew 11:28-29, emphasizing the simplicity of being a child of God.

   In Matthew 16:24, Jesus imparts wisdom about priorities. As time unfolds, the transient nature of worldly pursuits becomes evident. What endures eternally is our commitment to serving the Lord through Jesus. Jesus encourages us to reevaluate our priorities, shifting away from worldly concerns and aligning ourselves more closely with His teachings. Moving to Matthew 11:28-29, Jesus extends an invitation to those weary of the world's burdens. He assures His followers that a life dedicated to God the Father is inherently lighter than one focused solely on personal desires. Jesus contrasts the challenges of authentic Christian living with the burdens of a sinful life, affirming that submitting to God's will makes life more manageable. Psalm 37:4 emphasizes the necessity of wholeheartedly surrendering our hearts to God the Father. This entails relinquishing our sinful ways and genuinely striving to lead a righteous life, mirroring the example set by Jesus. In Psalm

37:5, the message is to entrust every aspect of our lives to God the Father and have faith that He has our best interests at heart.

(Free Writing)

10. In what way is the analogy of light brightening a dark room used to illustrate the changes people will see in you? Having a guiding light helps us navigate our surroundings without stumbling or getting hurt. When we live according to the Lord's guidance in a fallen world, we find success in all our endeavors, witness the fulfillment of our prayers at the right time, and receive every righteous desire bestowed by God.

(Free Writing)

11. What specific guidance does Psalm 37:3 provide for daily living on the Psalms Path? Devote yourself to dwelling in God's presence consistently every day, akin to the sheep grazing in the secure pasture of His care. Find safety in His grazing land, shielded from any powers of darkness. Make reading His holy scriptures a frequent practice, much like the daily nourishment your body receives through eating. Place greater trust in the Lord than in yourself and strive to embody goodness according to God's standards.

(Free Writing)

12. How is trust, as mentioned in the scripture, described as synonymous with believing? Place your trust in the Lord to a greater extent than in yourself, particularly because you will be co-creating a life that surpasses your physical capabilities.

    (Free Writing)

13. What role does Titus 3:14 play in emphasizing the value of dedicating ourselves to good works and aiding urgent needs?

    Christians must learn to devote themselves to doing what is good for others, not just themselves. The Lord wants to use us to help our family with urgent needs.

    (Free Writing)

14. How does Jeremiah 15:16 contribute to the understanding of feeding on God's faithfulness, and why is it compared to the nourishment of our spirits?

    Consider the act of reading scripture as a means of nourishing our spirits, akin to how consuming food nurtures our bodies. Additionally, acknowledge that God is the ultimate source of joy, surpassing everything else.

    (Free Writing)

15. Why does God emphasize not fretting three times in Psalm 37 (verses one, seven, and eight), and what does it indicate about facing challenges on the Psalms Path?

    It's not a matter of *if* we will face an attack from Satan, but *when*. The Lord desires us to be vigilant and spiritually prepared, ready to align our actions with His will. This preparation enables us to withstand the attack without succumbing to worry, ultimately enhancing the likelihood of witnessing our righteous desire come to fruition.

    (Free Writing)

16. What does Psalm 37:7 advise regarding the timeline for witnessing success and the need for patience?

    The Lord instructs us to wait patiently for Him to fulfill His promises to us. Expect it to take longer than you anticipate.

    (Free Writing)

17. How does the scripture instruct us to handle impatience in Psalm 37:7, and what caution does it offer?

Rejoice consistently, maintain a continuous prayer life, and express gratitude in all situations. Impatience may lead to fretting, jeopardizing our faith in the Lord. It's crucial not to succumb to fretting and instead to trust in God's timing.

(Free Writing)

18. In the waiting period mentioned in the Psalms Path, what encouragement does the scripture provide when facing challenges and observing others prospering?

You may observe others achieving success while facing challenges in the pursuit of your righteous desire. Recognize that this is a tactic of Satan to induce fretting and to sow doubt in the Lord's goodness. Succumbing to fretting can hinder the realization of your righteous desire.

(Free Writing)

19. According to the Psalms Path, why is it crucial to recognize challenges and successes as part of the Psalms Path?

Acknowledging that obstacles are inevitable is crucial for your ability to find rest in the Lord and to refrain from fretting about the process or timelines.

(Free Writing)

20. What role does faith play in the scriptures provided during the journey, such as Hebrews 11:1 and James 1:2-4?

    Jesus tells us that anything is possible for those who believe. Faith is literally that important. Anything is possible.

    (Free Writing)

21. Explain the significance of recognizing that the Lord's will cannot be thwarted by external forces, as mentioned in the Psalms Path.

    Fretting poses the most significant threat as you journey along the Psalms Path. It's likely why the Lord admonishes us against fretting three times within just eight scriptures.

    (Free Writing)

22. How does Psalm 37:8 advise individuals navigating the Psalms Path regarding anger and fretting?

    Do not fret. It's your biggest threat to your success.

    (Free Writing)

23. According to Psalm 37:5, what form of daily worship does the Lord encourage for those seeking righteous rewards?

    Rejoice always, pray continuously, and give thanks in all circumstances. This is the opposite of fretting. As stated in 1 Thessalonians 5:16-18 (NKJV), *"Rejoice always, pray without ceasing, in everything give thanks; for this is the will of God in Christ Jesus for you."*

    (Free Writing)

24. How does fretting impact the pursuit of righteous desires, and what perspective does the content offer on obstacles within the Psalms Path?

    It will cause you to doubt the Word of God. This is your biggest threat to seeing your righteous desire become your reality.

    (Free Writing)

25. In facing obstacles along the Psalms Path, what importance is placed on accepting setbacks and challenges, as mentioned in Isaiah 55:8-9?

    Stop trying to figure out your Psalms Path. Trying to institute your will while on your path will cause you to fret. Do not fret. You must accept that God is your only hope. Rest in that fact.

    (Free Writing)

26. How does James 1:2-4 contribute to the understanding of joy in facing trials and challenges within the context of spiritual maturity?

You should understand that obstacles are there to produce good spiritual fruit in you. When the time is right you will be an amazing warrior for God. A disciple of Jesus who lacks nothing.

(Free Writing)

27. What is the significance of acknowledging human reactions to obstacles and responding with obedience to God's commands in overcoming life's challenges (James 1:2-4)?

No one is telling you to stop being human. You will undoubtedly have reactions to your challenges and evil attacks of various kinds. The Lord has everything figured out. When you look back on your Psalms Path, you will realize it was perfect.

(Free Writing)

28. In what ways does the content advocate for a calm spirit of obedience to God's commands as individuals navigate through life's obstacles?

When you walk the Psalms Path the way the Lord intended, you will spiritually rest your way through the whole journey.

(Free Writing)

29. Why does God allow us to co-create righteous desires?

God loves us so much that He will grant us a righteous desire which we are allowed to co-create for the purpose of taking us from Christians to disciples. Because Christians are great, but disciples change the world.

(Free Writing)

Chapter 11
Enlightened Transcendence

Everything is about to make perfect sense as you understand your true identity as a disciple of Jesus. To help us understand our earthly life, Jesus gives us the parable of the ten minas, found in Luke 19:11-27.

<u>The Parable of the Ten Minas</u>

Luke 19:11-27 (NIV)

While they were listening to this, he went on to tell them a parable, because he was near Jerusalem and the people thought that the kingdom of God was going to appear at once.

He said: "A man of noble birth went to a distant country to have himself appointed king and then to return.

"So he called ten of his servants and gave them ten minas. 'Put this money to work,' he said, 'until I come back.'

"But his subjects hated him and sent a delegation after him to say, 'We don't want this man to be our king.'

"He was made king, however, and returned home. Then he sent for the servants to whom he had given the money, in order to find out what they had gained with it.

"The first one came and said, 'Sir, your mina has earned ten more.'

"'Well done, my good servant!' his master replied. 'Because you have been trustworthy in a very small matter, take charge of ten cities.'

"The second came and said, 'Sir, your mina has earned five more.' His master answered, 'You take charge of five cities.'

> "*Then another servant came and said, 'Sir, here is your mina; I have kept it laid away in a piece of cloth.*
>
> "'*I was afraid of you, because you are a hard man. You take out what you did not put in and reap what you did not sow.*'
>
> "*His master replied, 'I will judge you by your own words, you wicked servant! You knew, did you, that I am a hard man, taking out what I did not put in, and reaping what I did not sow?*
>
> "'*Why then didn't you put my money on deposit, so that when I came back, I could have collected it with interest?*'
>
> "*Then he said to those standing by, 'Take his mina away from him and give it to the one who has ten minas.*'
>
> "'*Sir,' they said, 'he already has ten!*'
>
> "*He replied, 'I tell you that to everyone who has, more will be given, but as for the one who has nothing, even what they have will be taken away.*
>
> "'*But those enemies of mine who did not want me to be king over them—bring them here and kill them in front of me.*'"

Here's the essence of what the minas parable means for you as you walk along the Psalms Path:

When we embrace Jesus' sacrifice and recognize Him as the Son of God, we are saved and adopted as children by our heavenly Father. In the parable, we are likened to servants, and the minas symbolize portions of the Lord's Holy Spirit. The Lord entrusts us with these portions of His Spirit, expecting us to utilize them according to our capabilities, with the assurance that they cannot be lost through use.

The servant who received a portion but hid it is criticized as being lazy and wicked. While Christians who conceal God's Spirit will still inherit His kingdom, they may not receive additional responsibilities. Therefore, let's aim not to be inactive servants but instead strive to be disciples who deeply grasp our identity in God's kingdom as both His children and servants.

Our Lord values labor and considers it commendable. He continually works in our lives out of delight, not obligation, recognizing the worth of labor itself. As responsible servants, we should cherish our share of the Holy Spirit, regarding it as precious treasure. Let's actively participate in His work, finding joy and fulfillment in doing so.

Moreover, the portion of the Holy Spirit given to each child of God is inexhaustible. It's intended for us to share freely, and as we do, we'll receive even more. There's no way for us to deplete the Lord's Spirit. Let's be servants who take our initial portion of His Holy Spirit, utilize it, and yield five times what we were given, or emulate the servant who transforms one portion into ten.

Righteous desires aren't just a choice; they're a fundamental principle of God's kingdom. It's crucial to pursue and abide within these desires. We're tasked with stewarding our spiritual gifts, using them for God's good purposes. This practice lightens our burdens, eases our lives, aligns our finances, and nurtures flourishing relationships based on His righteousness.

—

Embrace this new identity the Lord has already given you, leaving behind pursuits solely focused on earthly matters, where *you* sit on the throne of your life. Instead, step into the fullness of your identity in Christ, where *Jesus* reigns on the throne of your life. As you do so, you'll find that your burdens lighten, as the Lord adds no trouble to the endeavors of His disciples. This is not to say that your life will be a life of ease, but rather an abundant life, a life beyond the ordinary, a life extraordinary. Top of Form

Maybe you've felt weighed down by burdens—strained relationships, a stagnant career, a struggling business, a troubled marriage, or an addiction seeming insurmountable. But here's the truth: every setback ends now! In Jesus' name, claim your rightful place as a beloved child in our heavenly Father's kingdom. Embrace the righteous desires God has placed in you, meant to lift you from mere Christianity to a fervent disciple of Jesus, ablaze with holy fire, ready to bring change to your life and the world.

Let's pray:

Father God, thank You so much for loving me, saving me, and sharing Your Holy Spirit with me. Thank You for giving me Your Holy Bible, which I will use every day for the rest of my life to study Jesus, emulating everything He taught us. I accept my portion of Your Holy Spirit, reclaiming any that may be on deposit with Your bankers. I pray You will bless me as I move into my position as an elevated disciple of Jesus, actively using my portion of Your Holy Spirit to change the world around me for Your glory, kingdom, and good purposes. Lord Jesus, please take Your rightful place on the throne of my life. I love You. I thank You. In Jesus' name, amen.

Congratulations on your new life. Praise our Father God. We are so excited that you have claimed your rightful place in our Lord's kingdom. It's time to move forward.

Below is an exercise essential for your growth. I've included a sample worksheet, along with blank ones for you to periodically complete as you develop into your full identity as a disciple of Jesus.

Place each of your earthly things on the right side of the work sheet. This includes people, places, and things you have in your life. If you have multiple vehicles, place them separately. If you are married, place *spouse* on the right side of the paper. If you have a girlfriend/boyfriend, place them on the right side of the paper. If you have a spouse and are involved in an extramarital relationship, place them on the right side of the paper.

If you have multiple houses, place them separately on the right side of the paper. Look to the example and fill out everything in your earthly life on the right side.

LET'S CONNECT!

We're ready to serve you. If you're a disciple in need of counseling, simply scan this QR code to schedule a consultation with us.

If you own or aspire to own a business and desire tailored Psalms Path consulting for success, scan this QR code to begin your journey with us.

The purpose of this exercise:

When we are effective disciples of Jesus, everything listed within our earthly concerns on the right side, labeled "<u>Me</u>" and pertaining to this world, should free of unnecessary trouble. You should not have to overly dwell on these matters. This grants you more free time to do whatever the Lord lays on your heart to do.

Review the items listed on the right side of the paper. If you're not concerned about paying for your house or apartment, please draw a line through it, similar to the example provided.

If you enjoy a strong relationship with your spouse or child, please draw a line through each of them. Similarly, if your car is fully paid for, or you don't have to worry about payments or financial upkeep for it, also put a line through it.

Please draw lines through any items listed on the right side of the paper that you don't have to worry about. However, if you do have concerns regarding relationships, monthly payments, or similar matters, do not draw lines through those items.

Exercise Example (1)

God	Me
Saved/Christian	Spouse
Go to church on occasion	House
Tithe	Vehicle
	Vehicle
	Vehicle
	Vehicle
	Business
	Child
	Child
	Credit Card
	Credit Card
	Utilities
	Vacations
	Sports
	Entertainment
	Parent
	Parent
	Sibling

This example reflects a Christian who has trouble with the following:
- Relationships aren't the best, or are bad.
- House payment is a burden.
- Three vehicles which are tough to keep up with the payments and proper maintenance.
- Credit cards are maxed out and barely making the minimum payment.
- Utilities are tough to pay for.
- Goes on vacation on a credit card.
- Spends too much time on sports.
- Spends too much time on entertainment.

Exercise Example (1)

God	Me
Saved/Christian	~~Spouse~~
Understand that I'm a disciple	~~House~~
Chasing righteous desires	~~Vehicle~~
Living inside righteous desires	~~Vehicle~~
	~~Vehicle~~
Daily devotion	~~Vehicle~~
Pray daily	~~Business~~
Go to church	~~Child~~
Tithe from my first of my labor	~~Child~~
	~~Credit Card~~
Display fruits of the Spirit	~~Credit Card~~
Give of my time	~~Utilities~~
Give of my expertise	~~Vacations~~
Donate monthly to hungry children	~~Sports~~
	~~Entertainment~~
Do Facebook Live events for discipleship	~~Parent~~
	~~Parent~~
Writing a godly book	~~Sibling~~
Creating New Righteous Desire business	

- This disciple of Jesus enjoys great relationships, a house payment they can easily afford, vehicles that are easy to afford and maintain, a business that is profitable, great relationships with their family, and friends. They live in godly freedom with all the Lord has placed in their hands and do a ton of things guided by the Holy Spirit.

God	Me

Printed in the USA
CPSIA information can be obtained
at www.ICGtesting.com
LVHW021157041224
798233LV00004B/146